THE POWER OF SMILING

Using Positive
Psychology for Optimal
Health & Healing

The Spiritual Strengths Healing Plan

Richard P. Johnson, Ph.D.

ISBN 978-0-9895130-4-3

10 9 8 7 6 5 4 3 2 1

First Edition

Maggie Singleton, Editor

Cover design by Megan Irwin

Printed in the United States of America

BOOKS IN THE SPIRITUAL STRENGTHS HEALING SERIES

by Richard P. Johnson

- God Give Me Strength! Finding the Inner Power to Turn Your Illness/Brokenness/Life Transition Around

- Discover Your Spiritual Strengths: Find Health, Healing, and Happiness (flagship book of the Spiritual Strengths Healing Plan)

- Body, Mind, Spirit: Tapping the Healing Power Within

- Prayers for Spiritual Strength: Physical Illnesses, Emotional Broken Places, and/or Spiritual Dis-eases

- The Ten Most Effective Self-Care Healing Techniques: What You Can Do to Maximize Your Healing Journey

- The Power of Smiling: Using Positive Psychology for Optimal Health & Healing

- Healing Wisdom: 101 Spiritual Truths for Healing Your Illness

- Healing and Depression: Finding Peace in the Midst of Transition, Turmoil, or Illness

- Staying Spiritually Centered for Optimal Healing: Even When You're Sick or Life Seems Out of Control

- Seeking Significance: How to Discover New Self-Direction and New Life-Purpose Beyond Your (Unwanted) Life Transition

Caregiving Titles

- Caregiving from Your Spiritual Strengths: The Ten Fundamental Principles for Optimal Success

- Because I Care...Inspiration for Caregiving for Spouses, Health Care Personnel, Family & Friends

Foreword

This book takes the best of what positive psychology tells us about optimal living and connects it with the illness journey experience.

This book is intended for—

1. Persons with illness who wish to investigate methods and means (in addition to the medical realm) to help heal their illness.

2. Persons whose illness is currently in remission and who want to remain illness free.

3. Caregivers of persons with illness who wish to bring the very best possible to the healing path of persons with illness.

This book is best used as a companion to the Spiritual Strengths Healing Plan.

It would be immensely powerful for you to take the Spiritual Strengths Healing Profile (SSHP) sometime through your journey of this little book. The SSHP will give you insights into yourself that will allow these pages to come alive and truly bring positive change into your life.

Learn more at www.spiritualstrengthshealing.com.

The Spiritual Strengths Healing Plan

The Spiritual Strengths Healing Plan allows you to harness your internal healing power! It is not "faith healing" in which one relies on divine intervention as the sole means for physical cure, nor does it promise cure. Its purpose is healing and is best seen as a supplement to and support for current medical practices. The Spiritual Strengths Healing Plan's philosophy holds that each individual needs to seek the best and most appropriate medical and psychological care they can, in accord with their own personal wishes, and supplement their care with this Plan.

Please note that you will see the word "illness" throughout this book in its broadest sense and may indicate any (or a combination) of the following:

I. Physical Sicknesses

Cancer, heart disease, MS, Lupus, migraine, addictions, hypochondriasis, pain, weight management/loss, smoking cessation, pneumonia, COPD, hypertension, arthritis, immune disorders, Parkinson's, diabetes, stroke, chronic fatigue etc., etc.

II. Psychological Issues

Anxiety, depression, personality disorders, OCD, manipulation, stress, bi-polar disorder, etc., etc.

III. Emotional Issues

Being unrealistic, lacking responsibility, low-self-esteem, career focus issues, poor organization skills, family disharmony, anger management, fears, perfectionism, marriage discontent, lifelessness, infidelity, irritability, chronic lateness, caregiving, etc., etc.

IV. Spiritual Dis-eases

Peace of mind and heart, un-forgiveness, existential angst, inner pain, grudges, scrupulosity, incomplete developmental transitions, guilt, grief and unresolved grief, regrets, blame, disappointments, so-called "unfinished business," resentments, etc., etc.

V. Spiritual Direction & Growth

Gaining better clarity of God's plan in your life, and breaking through barriers that may be hindering your faith journey.

Where do you need healing?

For more information about the Spiritual Strengths Healing Plan, log on to...

www.SpiritualStrengthsHealing.com

The Spiritual Strengths Healing Institute

Learning the art of healing for self and others

Contents

Introduction

*Sometimes your joy is the source of your smile,
but sometimes your smile can be the source of your
joy.*

Thich Nhat Hanh

Positive psychology is the scientific study of well-being; it's a unique and contemporary sub-discipline of psychology that focuses on what contributes to, not detracts from, human happiness. Positive psychology is a relatively new branch of traditional psychology. Certainly Norman Vincent Peale, in his world renowned book The Power of Positive Thinking, served as a vanguard to the sub-discipline of positive psychology. Other authors, notably Salvatore Maddi, Ph.D. and Suzanne Kobasa, Ph.D. in their landmark book The Hardy Executive: Health Under Stress exposed other aspects of what was to become positive psychology.

It wasn't until Professor Martin Seligman, Ph.D. at the University of Pennsylvania produced vigorous, hard-data research that clearly demonstrated the value of what he termed "positive psychology," did it become a respectable scion of the more staid trunk of traditional psychology. Positive psychology is now universally seen as a practical framework for motivating positive challenge and peak performance. Today, Dr. Seligman is the recognized champion of positive psychology. He seeks to answer the question, the question, "what allows some people to live optimally?" in his book Learned Optimism, How to Change Your Mind and Your Life. He asks why some people seem to consistently—

- Move forward with optimism.
- Expect good things to happen.
- Find something to be grateful for.
- Notice beauty even in the bleakest of times.
- Acknowledge the "good stuff" of living.
- Give of themselves to others.
- Tolerate stress.
- Smile more easily.
- Have strong life principles that guide them.
- Snap out of "bad" situations or moods.
- Live more alert, active, and fulfilling lives.

Traditional psychology has been criticized almost from its beginnings as being too "pathology oriented," that is, trying to discover what was "wrong" with a person, a relationship, an organization, and the like. Consequently, clinical psychology has developed a mammoth lexicon of "mental illnesses" all codified in the Diagnostic and Statistical Manual, 5th Edition (DSM). The DSM is a comprehensive, even exhaustive, tome that attempts to pinpoint each and every variant of "abnormal" human behavior and describe each in detail so that all clinicians of psychology can speak the same language.

The effort is certainly a noble and necessary one, yet by only describing abnormal behavior and ignoring the best of what the human species can generate, it seems to skew all human behavior in a negative direction. Traditional psychology starts with the question, *"Why is the person feeling so badly?"* and tries to develop therapies to move the person to a more stable state of normalcy.

The emergence of positive psychology may be seen as a reaction against the mental illness-oriented assumptions of traditional psychology by attempting to validate high level, even peak performance and excellence in human behavior. Positive psychology is not interested in normalcy; rather it's interested in why some people seem so mentally healthy, hardy, vigorous, and vital well beyond the "norm."

Focus on What's Right about a Person

Instead of looking for what is "wrong," positive psychology focuses on what is "right" and strong and stable and energizing about the person who is functioning very well, even extremely well, and who claims to feel exceptionally good, even when they are sick. Positive psychology seeks to discover the unique factors and forces that allow this person to stand out as one who is clearly buoyant of mood, clear of vision, creative of thought, optimistic of emotions, effective in problem solving, and decisive in action.

This fundamental notion of positive psychology is perfectly aligned with the primary assumption of the *Spiritual Strengths Inner Healing Plan.* The beginning centerpiece of the *Spiritual Strengths Healing Plan* is the Spiritual Strengths Healing Profile (SSHP), a 120-item questionnaire that identifies an individual's six "premier" spiritual strengths...the unique, and personality-specific combination of God's healing power (grace) that resides within an individual (see www.spiritualstrengthshealing.com to find out more about the SSHP and to take it online).

If there are "secrets" to health, healing, and happiness within each of us, these "secrets" are our six spiritual strengths.

Because positive psychology investigates what's "right" about us, what makes us feel better and do our best, a key factor of positive psychology is reframing what otherwise might be seen as human foibles (brokenness) into potentially unique contributions to vital living. Again, this is exactly what the *Spiritual Strengths Healing Plan* accomplishes as it first identifies our, 1) shadows and, 2) compulsions, and then instructs us, through a marvelous journey of self-understanding, to frame these "personal foibles" as personality markers, which always point to our spiritual strengths. Simply put, what were formerly seen as personal weaknesses are transformed into spiritual personality clues that help us unearth our innate spiritual strengths—namely God's healing and animating grace operating within us.

Smiling: The Best of Positive Psychology

Positive psychology, illness, and smiling may sound like strange bedfellows indeed, but when we look closer we find some surprising connections. Of all the tools in positive psychology's toolbox, smiling is perhaps the easiest to perform, the quickest acting, and the most effective in bringing about the tremendously positive effects discovered by positive psychology research...and one that is sorely needed throughout the illness journey.

Can smiling have an effect on our personalities? Can smiling have a positive effect upon illness? Psychological research that looks at the effects of smiling all seems to arrive at a universal conclusion: **smiling is the key to a positive outlook on life.** The positive effects of smiling are legion: improved immune function, increased tolerance for pain and frustration, lowered stress and blood pressure, and even higher levels of creativity. Dr. Robert Ammens of the University of California at Davis and Dr. Michael McCulloch at the University of Miami have documented surprising results of regularly practicing the tools of positive psychology. These results include being less materialistic; more generous; less depressed, anxious, and envious; and being more empathetic, helpful, energetic, determined, joyful, and strong. Such persons also experienced clearer thinking, increased resilience, fewer illnesses, and reported living less cluttered lives.

Interestingly, and very importantly, the positive effects of smiling are seen whether the smile is genuine or "forced." Evidently the mind doesn't know the difference and reacts similarly to either.

Research also points to the fact that smiling has dramatic effects on personal interactions. Smiling seems to increase altruism; smiling people simply get more help/aid/assistance from others. Smiling people are more attractive and approachable than they otherwise would be.

The Power of Smiling

Dr. Mark Stibich, Ph.D. offers us ten general ways that smiling affects us positively: relationally, emotionally, behaviorally, and psychologically.

See http://longevity.about.com/od/lifelongbeauty/tp/smiling.htm for more information. Smiling—

1. Makes us attractive. We are drawn to people who smile. Frowns, scowls, and grimaces all push people away, but a smile draws them in.

2. Changes our mood. It's hard to be "moody" when we're wearing a smile. A smile can "trick" our bodies into shifting our mood in a positive direction.

3. Is contagious. A smile brightens up all those around us; it makes our lives happier.

4. Relieves stress. Smiling saves us from appearing tired, worn down, and overwhelmed—all of which increase our internal stress levels.

5. Boosts our immune system. Our immune system is hyper-sensitive to our mood; when we smile, we boost our mood which also strengthens our immune system making us less vulnerable to everything from colds and flu to infections of all types—even illness.

6. Lowers our blood pressure. When we reduce our stress, we experience a corresponding decrease in hypertension (high blood pressure).

7. Releases endorphins, natural painkillers, and serotonin. All of these are chemicals that our bodies naturally produce. Endorphins increase our overall sense of well-being. Natural painkillers fight pain of all types, and serotonin regulates our mood.

8. Injects more tone, freshness, and vibrancy into our appearance. Smiling shapes our faces in such a way that we look younger. Smiling works like a natural face lift. Smiling is an anti-gravity "miracle drug" that re-sculpts our facial muscles and gives us a new vitality.

9. Makes us seem successful. Smiling raises our confidence level, gives us enhanced self-esteem, and improves our overall poise; all these give us an air of success.

10. Helps us stay positive. Smiling is our best "attitude adjustment." It's hard to think of something negative when we're smiling.

Smiling Can Change Your Personality

How can we combine the best of positive psychology with the enlightened quest of smiling to create a new climate for healing our illness or vitalizing our caregiving? Smiling does seem to bring about personality change in a positive direction. The change potential of a smile can be experienced either internally or externally. Internally, smiling offers much. It can—

- Generate a new mental attitude.
- Bring about a change in insight or outlook.
- Shift our thoughts from negative to positive.
- Stimulate new, more positive emotional reactions.
- Activate new choices that bring personality growth.
- Move us to action.

External changes are those that other people can see. While our attitudes, perceptions, thoughts, feelings, and even our decisions lay hidden beneath the surface, others *do* see our behaviors and actions...what we do! So smiling has the power to actually change our behavior! This change is most important because it's only by our actions (behavior) that others come to see us, engage with us, and evaluate us. Fortunately or not, we're judged by our actions.

Let's look at some of the basic tenets of positive psychology and see how they may interface with smiling.

The Basic Tenets of Positive Psychology Correlated with Smiling

Positive psychologists have discovered smiling is a powerful tool that can—

1. Shift our basic beliefs from ones of scarcity to ones of abundance. A smile can move us away from deficits in ourselves and toward a search for our strengths. Smiling can shift our vision so that instead of seeing potential obstacles, we now see challenges that are intrinsically motivating.

2. Help re-draw a new picture of living that galvanizes our attention and vitalizes our unique resources.

3. Develop a "strengths vision" so we can see what is creative, what is resourceful, and what is integrated in us. Smiling lets us see a more global picture, and accents the positive traits and creative qualities in our personality.

4. Focus our mind's eye to see what's "worked" for us in the past and shape our efforts around these motivated abilities.

5. Help us speak from our "strengths voice" and speak to our own internal "strengths receptors."

6. Allow us to appreciate what thrills us; a smile offers us a sense of awe, wonder, and delight. A smile activates us to use our own emotional intelligence so we can engage in a search for those emotions that energize and animate us, rather than focusing on those emotions that paralyze us.

7. Lets us generate "action options" that "move and stir" our core desires and develop goals that create challenge, objectives that serve the goals, and strategies for achieving all this.

8. Promote personal engagement. Smiling helps us animate our desires into action; a smile allows us to always be "working on" improving ourselves.

9. Helps us live in the eternal NOW.

Personal Meaning

Our overall goal in life, and this is particularly true during our illness journey, is to position ourselves so we can achieve ever-higher and deeper levels of personal meaning. Personal meaning is our heart's desire...we crave it. Personal meaning comes primarily from being in ever deeper relationships with others and with God. In a sense, smiling propels us toward a new arena of meaning that enhances our relationships with others and consequently brings us closer to our true selves.

When we use smiling to inject the basic tenets of positive psychology into our lives, we better position ourselves to find new levels of fulfillment. We elevate our healing and enrich our lives because we're continuously looking for "what's good" and not "what's wrong." In the process, we become better. We discover the packet of wonder, God's healing grace inside of us, and come to a place of animated wholeness most conducive to healing. Smiling helps us open up the windows to our soul so that God's healing grace (one's spiritual strengths) can enter into us unrestricted by fear and ego to animate our entire being and set the stage for healing.

Types of Smiling

How many types of smiling are there? It turns out that there are several...and they all communicate a slightly different message. Way back in the nineteenth century, a French researcher by the name of Duchenne du Boulogne made a fundamental discovery about smiling. By stimulating various muscles in the face with a non-painful electric current, Duchenne was able to differentiate between two types of smiles. The first type of smile is one that conveys true happiness. Duchenne found that true happiness smiles were ones that involved the eyes, while other smiles that did not engage eye muscles might convey an emotion that was something less than happy. Today we name the total "happiness" smile a Duchenne smile, or simply "D-smile;" and those smiles that do not convey happiness [those with no discernible eye involvement] as "non D-smiles."

The distinction between D-smiles and non D-smiles is somewhat academic for our purposes. In healing, we're not so interested in the external consequences of our smile on others (as powerful as they are), as much as we're interested in the internal consequences of our smile, i.e., what's happening to us on the inside. When we view smiling from this internal vantage point, we can see that even the slightest smile has tremendous and positive internal rewards. Even in those most private, solitary, and personally intimate times, when some internal prompt sparks us to smile even the faintest smile…the one that might be hardly (if at all) noticeable, we put into motion a sequence of internal events that initiates a veritable cascade of health-giving and mood-elevating chemicals and hormones that shift our perspective, our thoughts, feelings, and our choices.

Smiling and Your Spiritual Life

Our smile literally moves us internally; our hearts are touched, and our personalities shift. But most curiously, this tiny smile is not insignificant on a spiritual level either. This most simple human action, the everyday action of a smile, generates the most immense effects. It opens up the portals of our real selves, the sacred doorways of God's power and might through which gush the celestial grace-power that is ever available to us, but which so many times we are indifferently or inadvertently unaware of. Even the most diminutive and common smile touches the innermost and tender parts of our inner core; it transforms us with the energy of heaven—that intangible place called our soul.

Richard P. Johnson, Ph.D.

Thirty-five Days to Replace Fear with Hope

In the following pages, I offer 35 "Smiling Truisms," which represent the fruit of my thought, prayer, and meditation on the impact of smiling on spiritual healing. I would like to suggest the following five-point method for using these 35 truisms...

1. Thoughtfully read through these 35 "smiling truisms."

2. Use them, and the descriptions, as prayer.

3. Meditate on the 35.

4. Use them on a daily basis, perhaps one per day, until you embrace them and let them enfold your heart.

5. Be with them, and they will become part of you.

A Final Note:

I am a Christian by birth and practice, and I have no doubt that this lifetime faith walk shows through in these pages. Please don't infer from this bias that this book is only for Christians. I believe that the truths in these pages are universal. I've written them from a Christian perspective because it's the only one that is natural for me. If you are not a Christian, then I ask you to filter my bias so that my words ring clear and true to you. I thank you.

Day One

When I smile, I remember my spiritual strengths.

God has invested "power and might" in me uniquely.

My job is to come to a clearer understanding of these most purposeful strengths and to do my very best to express them out to the world.

Smiling gives me pause to remember that indeed I have been endowed by God; I have been given God's "power and might" right here right now.

Smiling serves as my behavioral cue that I am continuously called to "be" in my spiritual strengths—to immerse myself in them and to saturate my personality with them.

A kind heart is a fountain of gladness, making everything in its vicinity freshen into smiles.

Washington Irving

Day Two

When I smile, I align myself with the divine power in me.

Smiling helps me "center" on God's presence in me.

Smiling helps me embrace that, *"Blessed is he who comes in the name of the Lord,"* refers to me and to everyone as representatives of Christ.

Smiling sends an internal message from God that travels on the unseen and unknown spiritual communication lines within me.

The message tells me that I am first and foremost a "child of God"—not just a "child of the world." This ever new and yet ever ancient identity is the truth of my soul.

Smiling helps me pull back from the frantic seeking of the world and the fearful grasping of my ego and to center instead on the presence of God within me.

A smile can brighten the darkest day.

Author Unknown

Day Three

When I smile, I can better feel and show God's internal calm.

The world offers no permanent calm, no true peace.

True peace comes only from God, animated by the Holy Spirit.

Smiling helps me find the rest that only God can give.

Smiling reminds me to put aside my agitation, my contention, my complexity, and my insecurities.

Smiling begins the healing process of replacing these unwanted intruders with the calm of the universe, the tenderness of the Blessed Mother, the compassion of the saints, and the silent quiet of the Holy Spirit.

All the statistics in the world can't measure the warmth of a smile.

Chris Hart

Day Four

When I smile, I can find my genuine voice.

I've been given a true voice, a voice that speaks from the depths of serenity, wisdom, and simplicity.

I am at my best when I speak from this true voice and not the many other voices that I've learned from the world.

Smiling helps me put aside the voice of anger and prejudice, of irritation and frustration, of timidity and neglect, and of arrogance and brutishness.

Smiling ushers me to a healing place where I can choose the true voice I've been given as gift.

This real voice is mine alone; it's the voice I need to use, and the voice that the world needs to hear.

When I speak with my real voice, I am speaking from my soul.

Keep smiling—it makes people wonder what you've been up to.

Author Unknown

Day Five

When I smile, I become more fully open to God's grace.

It's been said that grace falls on saint and sinner alike, but that saints hold up funnels and sinners hold up umbrellas.

I am both saint and sinner at the same time; I hold a funnel in one hand and an umbrella in the other!

Smiling helps me make the better choice.

I seek to be as open as possible to the power and might of grace.

God is the source of my energy; God's grace, animated by the Holy Spirit, is my only energy, and all energy (mine and everyone's) comes from this one source.

Smiling opens the portals of grace that I may have closed by my known commissions against, or my unknown omissions from, aligning my will with God's will for me.

Smiling helps me sensitize my spiritual receptor sites so that I'm ever ready to receive the abundance of God's grace.

A smile is something you can't give away, it always comes back to you.

Author Unknown

Day Six

When I smile, I find joy in living.

Jesus reminded us to be of good cheer, indeed to celebrate the richness of life in all its variegations.

While there is desolation in life, there is always the consolation of Christ.

Smiling signals me to remember the joy of living in Christ. It reminds me to surmount the dejection that can sometimes visit me.

Smiling moves me to reject the over-stimulation of the distractions of the world that masquerade as meaning but offer no joy.

Smiling helps me express happiness of heart; it activates my spiritual life force of universal love and offers me healing.

Smiling allows me a jubilant knowing that I am the recipient of God's consoling, healing, and powerful grace.

Smiling lets me luxuriate in being "wonder filled" by God.

A laugh is a smile that bursts.

Mary H. Waldrip

Day Seven

When I smile my cares begin to melt away.

When I smile, my worries seem to erode a bit; dread of disaster begins to evaporate.

When I smile, fear slides off my shoulders and any sense of personal insufficiency drains from me forming a puddle on the floor below.

Smiling seems to emancipate me from guilt, and lifelessness, and rigidity, and indifference; smiling gifts me with healing.

Smiling spiritually lifts me up to stand straight and tall in God's presence within.

Smiling helps me to forget about my grasping self and focus instead on what's more real about me...my holy self.

It is almost impossible to smile on the outside without feeling better on the inside.

Author Unknown

Day Eight

When I smile, I can better focus on the "main thing."

Smiling reminds me to keep the "main thing" the "main thing."

Smiling sharpens my vision so I don't lose sight of what my life is all about.

Smiling helps me align the "right now" of my life with the "main event" of my life — God's steady pulse of life in me.

Smiling reminds me of my purpose. It helps me get back "on track" with the work of the Holy Spirit within me.

Smiling helps me lower the centerboard on my life sailboat so I can sail straight and secure.

Every day you spend without a smile, is a lost day.

Author Unknown

Day Nine

When I smile, I can think clearer.

I seek deeper and deeper meaning in life and smiling helps my thinking "make better meaning" from life.

Smiling reminds me to "connect the dots" of any situation, relationship, goal, interaction pattern, or enterprise of my life in such a way that aligns my personality with truth.

Smiling allows me to see every part of my life through the eyes of Christ.

Smiling helps me use the cognitive template of God's love as the most important schemata for "framing" what's happening in my life.

Smiling allows me to come to a clearer understanding of my ongoing growth toward Jesus.

Smiling is my cue to raise my awareness of the role of faith in my life and to think with the mind of Christ.

Smiling helps me begin to clear away any disturbing or distracting self-talk, and replace it with thoughts of peace and harmony.

Is a smile a question? Or is it the answer?

Lee Smith

Day Ten

When I smile, I start to feel better connected to God and to others.

Smiling triggers deeper connections between others and me, and fosters a more penetrating connection with God.

Connection with others is a requirement of my being; it's as necessary as the very air that I breathe.

Connection with God is my true heart's desire.

Smiling affords me the experience of true spiritual connection with others by helping me recognize that there is a "spiritual something" in me that is "in sync" with a similar "spiritual something" in another person.

Smiling ignites the intangible power that moves me closer to both God's children and to God as well.

Smiling lets me step back from my self-serving ways and see the Christ in another human being, indeed in every human being.

When this happens, I'm elevated to another plane of living, a plane that offers me a new vantage point on my life and a new discernment of spirit.

Smile—sunshine is good for your teeth.

Author Unknown

Day Eleven

When I smile, I can make better choices.

Choices are everywhere in my world—developing strategies, selecting goals and objectives, uncovering options, and constructing plans are all part of the personality function of making decisions.

Smiling gives me a quiet internal realization that the common everyday choices I make actually determine the kind of world I live in.

Smiling alerts me that I need never give away my free will choice to persons or forces that inhibit my forward spiritual growth.

Smiling gently nudges me toward aligning my will with God's will, and therein finding the healthiest and the most abundant way of living.

I am best when I choose God's way, God's relationship, and God's values as my guiding principles for living fully...smiling helps me in that quest.

Smile—it increases your face value.

Author Unknown

Day Twelve

When I smile, I act in peace and love.

People judge me by my actions, and I seek to act in the Lord when I am at my most noble and spiritual best.

Smiling gives me a moment so I have the "space" to quickly sort out my thoughts, feelings, and choices before I act.

This space, which smiling offers, gives me the peace in which I can sort out my next actions so I can act with the hands, and the feet, and the tongue of Christ, and not fumble with my own.

My behavior is my personal signature of "who" I am, not just a statement of "what" I am.

St. Paul says that, *"You can tell them by their fruits."* It's my behavior that shows others and me what I'm really made of.

When I act with the hands of God, I also act in peace and love.

Peace begins with a smile.

Blessed Mother Teresa

Day Thirteen

When I smile, I activate my internal healing system.

I know that the most powerful healing generator is right within me.

Medications, potions, exercise, stress reduction, healthy relationships are all factors in the equation for healing, but the glue that holds it all together is faith, and my smile confirms my bedrock faith.

Jesus always told the people whom he healed that it was their faith that healed them. I believe that Jesus smiled when he said those words.

Carrying a smile with me on my journey stimulates all the mechanisms for healing in me: my immune system, indeed all the systems of my body, my centered personality, my beliefs, attitudes and values, and much more.

In short, my smile pulls me toward that most valued gift from God...the gift of faith, the ultimate healing power there is.

No matter how grouchy you're feeling, you'll find the smile more or less healing.   It grows in a wreath all around the front teeth—thus preserving the face from congealing.

Anthony Ewer

Day Fourteen

When I smile, I better see what's real.

Who is in charge of my awareness?

What filter do I put in front of my vision that prevents me from seeing clearly?

Smiling helps me see clearer; it peels the cataracts off my spiritual eyes allowing me to see what's really "real" in me, in others, and in any situation.

I pause when I smile and gain in this moment a keener outlook and a sharper insight. I can see what is true, and genuine, and authentic when I look with my spiritual inner eye.

Smiling helps expand the lens of my awareness so I can take in the bigger picture of my existence.

My smile lets me see the contrails of love streaking across my view of the world.

It's here in this sublime panorama that I find the realest "real" in my reality...I see the celestial symmetry of Christ.

God smiles on our smiles.

Author Unknown

Day Fifteen

When I smile, I'm more attractive and approachable.

No doubt about it, people respond better to people who offer a smile.

People are more compliant with my wishes, more open to my thinking, and significantly more accepting of the fullness of me in every respect when I wear a smile.

My smile somehow reveals the glow of Christ in me; it illuminates my inner beauty, and demonstrates, as few other things can, the distinctiveness of my personality.

When I smile, I show my unique inner luster.

Smiling says that I'm "OK," that I'm accessible, reasonable, light, bright, and easy to be with.

Smiling motivates me and motivates others to be "in-sync" with me, and to be comfortable with me.

Happiness isn't the easiest thing to find, but one place you're guaranteed to find it is in a friend's smile.

Allison Poler

Day Sixteen

When I smile, I'm more the "real" me.

Whom am I really, whom is the "real" me?

Am I more "me" when I frown, or ridicule, or use sarcasm?

Smiling reminds me who I am at my core, at the center of the center of me.

Smiling allows me to function from that beautiful point of light within me, to feel the Spirit's soothing touch and warming glow, and to embrace (not with resignation or submission) my true nature and my true mission in life.

Smiling helps me to be more genuine, authentic, and transparent.

A genuine smile says, "I am what you see here. I have nothing to hide. I carry not pretenses, and I wear no masks. I am the real me!"

Smile, it is the key that fits the lock of everybody's heart.

Anthony D'Angelo

Day Seventeen

When I smile, I immediately feel better.

Like you, I always seek to feel good. I want to feel "up" and energetic, sharp and "with it," and positive and useful.

Smiling seems to put a shine on my day, a hop in my step, and an inspiration in my heart.

Feelings are the emotional "facts" of the moment, and a smile focuses on the most vitalizing emotional facts that are present in any situation if you look hard enough.

Smiling doesn't mean that I'm a fraud, that I'm a Pollyanna—always needing to see only the good things and only allowing positive feelings in.

Smiling energizes me so that I don't overlook those fantastic flashes of true reality, those intangible facets of the Presence of the Divine that elevate me and bring me home.

A smile helps me begin to understand the magnificence of wholeness in reality...and wholeness feels good!

The shortest distance between two people is a smile.

Author Unknown

Day Eighteen

When I smile, I synchronize my body chemistry toward balance and coherence.

Everything is attached to everything else; certainly all the various parts of me are all connected.

When I detach one part of me from the others, then the totality of me doesn't work as well.

Smiling helps bring me together; it reminds me to patiently observe the celestial order and symmetry that God has planted in me from the start.

Smiling brings the disparate parts of me together and into balance.

Smiling launches me into the restorative process of transformation, finding God's power in me, the power that re-makes me all new, as Christ promised.

I have a tickle in my brain. And it keeps making the corners of my mouth point toward the heavens.

Jeb Dickerson

Day Nineteen

When I smile, I'm better equipped to deal with whatever comes along.

Loss is woven into the fabric of living fully.

I've learned that I need loss; I can't grow without loss.

Smiling offers me a new strength of realizing that I am endowed with the necessary armor and the most powerful tools so I can accept whatever loss comes my way, and whatever diminishments may subtract from me.

Smiling moves me along the royal road to acceptance, which is my true "spiritual grit," the power and might of God that propels me through and beyond whatever trials and tribulations the world throws at me.

Smiling is my outward sign that my true self is impervious to harm; I may experience loss upon loss (like Job), but through it all, my smile is the face of God that I wear; my smile is the hand of God that is with me always and protects me from all evil.

If you don't start out the day with a smile, it's not too late to start practicing for tomorrow.

Author Unknown

Day Twenty

When I smile, I'm stronger.

In God, I am potent.

I am an effective change-agent for myself and for others.

Smiling sets my jaw so I can accept "attack" with vigor.

Smiling reminds me that I cannot be hurt.

Smiling awakens me to be straightforward and upright in action.

Smiling links me with the grace of self-discipline so I can "get through" what I need to, and achieve what I want to.

Smiling gives me the capacity for sustained action.

Smiling allows me to trust myself and take on risk that I might otherwise overlook.

My smile gives me a new sense of personal determination that allows me to carry forward even when I'm afraid.

A smile displays the immortal flow of energy that nourishes, extends, and preserves. It's the eternal goal in life.

Smiley Blanton

Day Twenty-one

When I smile, I can better see the goodness in others.

God's goodness is everywhere, yet it's very hard for me to see it consistently.

My smile reminds me to look closer at myself, at others, the world, and God, with the more understanding and forgiving eyes of Christ.

Smiling helps me look past the faults, the imperfections, the contradictions, and the frustrations that are so prevalent in the world, and in myself, and instead view a different reality just beyond the over-abundant brokenness of this plane.

My smile stimulates me to put on new eyes so I can see the truth, beauty, and goodness in everyone, regardless of how deep I need to look.

Smiling allows me to be fully present in this material plane and yet simultaneously present on the intangible plane as well.

Today, give a stranger one of your smiles; it might be the only sunshine he sees all day.

H. Jackson Brown

Day Twenty-two

When I smile, irritation and frustration begin to drain away.

I feel irritated and frustrated because I give myself thoughts that are not totally whole.

I get a distorted picture of reality because I can only see through the glass darkly.

Consequently I can form distorted thoughts from this distorted reality, which in turn generates irritation and frustration (and so many other paralyzing emotions).

When I put on a smile, I break this morbid cycle.

My smile soothes me; it calms my ragged emotions and lets me see through the glass clearer.

Smiling releases me from noxious emotions that contort my life, and lets me embrace uplifting emotions that animate my life.

Smiling gives me the freedom to be more than I thought I was.

Smiling lifts me up above the distractions of the world to a new emotional space of peace and calm.

A smile confuses an approaching frown.

Author Unknown

Day Twenty-three

When I smile, I'm more "in charge" of myself.

When I walk without my smile, I defensively give the direction for my life over to others.

Smiling offers me a hardy reliability and a steadfast self-agency so that I can act on my own and not forfeit my true self to people or forces outside myself.

Smiling gives me a renewed faith in myself as a competent person. Smiling lets me jettison that which tends to stop me, and take on that which tends to propel me.

Smiling helps me capture that I am a whole person fully capable of executing even challenging tasks with a smooth and yet decisive hand.

On the soul level, smiling reassures me that I am credible, strong, and courageous.

A smile is a curve that sets everything straight.

Phyllis Diller

Day Twenty-four

When I smile my pain and brokenness are easier to bear.

I am broken in ways both known and unknown to me.

Brokenness causes me pain on many levels: physical, emotional, familial, psychological, and/or spiritual.

Sometimes this brokenness threatens to overpower me, to take control of me.

Smiling lets me reclaim myself, lets me exert power over the pain and brokenness.

Smiling allows me to turn the tables as it were on the pain and brokenness, and once again take the reins of my life back, as opposed to letting pain of my brokenness control my life.

Smiling is my therapeutic antidote of choice for whatever life brings my way.

Naturally I want to consult with and use the tools of the medical community, yet if I do this with a frown rather than a smile, I undermine its potential benefit for me.

The world always looks brighter from behind a smile.

Author Unknown

Day Twenty-five

When I smile, I'm more forgiving.

To err is human, but to forgive truly is divine.

When I forgive, I rise above the merely human part of me and touch the divine in me.

Smiling helps me not only remember that forgiveness of others, and of myself, is always an option; but in addition, smiling actually helps me to move from a mere my intention to forgive all the way to the action of forgiving.

Smiling helps me overcome the many blocks that I can put in the way of forgiving.

Smiling allows me to break through my prejudices and offer my total "amen" to the person I forgive.

Smiling gets me past my distorted need for personal recompense.

Smiling straightens my irrational thinking that things like this simply shouldn't happen at all.

Every time you smile at someone, it is an action of love, a gift to that person, a beautiful thing.

Blessed Mother Teresa

Day Twenty-six

When I smile, I'm more resilient.

Smiling helps me use the traits, skills, and abilities necessary to bounce back from disruptive change.

Smiling aids me in developing a new set of survivor skills that allow me to thrive under the chaos of constant change.

Smiling assists me in honoring my most effective global characteristic that distinguishes between the me who stands up straight to the rigors of life, and the me who simply avoids, submits, becomes depressed, and/or throws his hands up in exasperation.

Smiling helps me revel in change and become even better than what I was before.

Smiling prevents me from gradually unraveling under the stress that life throws my way.

Smiling helps me derive meaning from adversity and use my God-given resources, both internal and external, to foster continuing growth.

A friendly look, a kindly smile, one good act, and life's worthwhile.

Author Unknown

Day Twenty-seven

When I smile, I invite the Holy Spirit into my life.

The Holy Spirit showers me with the grace I need to persevere.

Smiling activates my awareness that the Holy Spirit is always with me.

Smiling generates an expectation in me that the power that I don't think I have is actually available if I simply trust in God.

Smiling stimulates a new openness in me to better invigorate the gifts of the Holy Spirit...gifts that I know that I have but which need to be invited out of my heart into the open.

Smiling helps me pry open my soul and let the Holy Spirit's abundant power and might gush in and gush out.

A smile is the universal welcome.

Max Eastman

Day Twenty-eight

When I smile, I can put my best foot forward.

The real me aches to get out of the confinement that I have constructed as its enclosure for far too long.

I'm the one that forges the chains that hold the best of me inside.

Smiling helps release the bonds that bind my best gifts and strengths inside me.

Smiling sets my strengths free from the captivity of self-abasement, self-forfeiture, and submissiveness...all of which are bars forming a cage around me.

Smiling lets me find the truth in me, so I can recognize the honesty and truth that pulsates deep in me and yearns to be free.

Smiling rescues the best of me from a prison of self-neglect and timidity.

A smile is an inexpensive way to change your looks.

Charles Gordy

Day Twenty-nine

When I smile, I'm a better person.

I know that I am better than what I commonly offer to the world.

There is so much more of me that I find so difficult to show.

My light has never really burned as bright as it could.

Smiling gives me a stage upon which I can better express the best of me.

Smiling offers a new frame for me that accents all that's good, and right, and bright, and beautiful in me.

My smile showcases the best qualities that reside in me and which I seldom bring to the surface.

Smiling gives me entrée into the hearts and minds of others, a pathway to fulfillment and purpose that has escaped me for far too long.

A smile is the light in the window of your face that tells people you're at home.

Author Unknown

Day Thirty

When I smile, I'm more sensitive to others and to myself.

How much more there is in others and in me that I have overlooked because I so often fail to practice the simple task of smiling.

I want to discover deeper understanding of myself and of others.

I want to be closer to others and more present to myself.

I want to experience the passion of life at its depths.

Smiling gives me so much more of life than I could know otherwise; and it does this so simply and yet so powerfully.

Smiling opens my emotions so I not only know the facts of those with whom I work and play, but their inner life as well.

Smiling helps me go far beyond the facts of living, to the central feelings of living, the real "stuff" of life...to the effective affect of living.

If you smile at someone, they might smile back.

Author Unknown

Day Thirty-one

When I smile, I'm in "celebration mode."

My smile says that I not only see my gifts and the gifts of others, but I celebrate them.

My smile holds up the best of everything that exists everywhere.

Today my smile generates gratitude in ways I only wished for yesterday.

My smile is like raising my arms in praise for the wonder of all of life.

Smiling makes me overflow with appreciation, almost burst with delight for all of life.

Smiling brings me all of this and so much more that I can't even express in words.

Smiling elevates me to be overcome with the joy of living, the wonder of the Presence of God, and the exuberance of knowing that the Holy Spirit is in and all about me.

Life is like a mirror; we get the best results when we smile at it.

Author Unknown

Day Thirty-two

When I smile, I'm reminded to live in the simplicity of the here and now.

There is an honest and humble sacredness right in my midst at this very moment.

My smile awakens me to this awareness; it gives me pause to consider the truth, beauty, and goodness that pulsate in everything everywhere.

My smile invites me to participate in the power of the divine that innervates the "All" of the cosmos.

The fingerprint of heaven rests on all things, all people, all relationships, and all endeavors, and my smile helps me look deep enough so I can see it.

My smile prepares me to see the grandeur of all that is.

Everyone smiles in the same language.

Author Unknown

Day Thirty-three

When I smile, I am brought to prayerfulness.

As I walk the corridors and the pathways of my life today, my smile reminds me to be in communion with the divine power that pulsates within me always.

My smile helps me remember that the divine is closer to me than the air that I breathe.

Smiling saturates me in continual prayer, a state of being that I long to become my new way of working, my new way of living, and my new way of being.

Smiling lets me thrive in the trueness of me.

Smiling helps me to be totally active in my everyday tasks while at the same time immersed with and in the divine.

A smile is a powerful weapon; you can even break ice with it.

Author Unknown

Day Thirty-four

When I smile, I feel energized.

My smile activates a jolt of joy that pulsates through my body, mind, and soul like an uplifting impulse of energy.

My smile reminds me that I am part of the greatness of creation, and that all I encounter today is as well.

My smile-induced joy allows me to see beyond what formerly snagged my mind and heart and brought me "down."

My smile lets me see the beauty that's right in front of me ...beauty that I may have otherwise overlooked.

My smile ignites an updraft of inspiration and a free-spirited lightness in me that propels me forward with a renewed determination and a refortified confidence.

Smiling animates me in joy, which elevates my heart; it gives me a positive attitude and an inner balance knowing that God's grace sustains me always.

I've never met a smiling face that was not beautiful.

Author Unknown

Day Thirty-five

When I smile, I know that I'm not alone.

Smiling helps me remember that even in times of discouragement, pain, and/or turmoil (especially in these times) that I am never alone: God will not abandon me.

Smiling helps me confidently confront rough times knowing that God is by my side...always!

Smiling reminds me that there is so much more to living than the "details" of life, and that that "more" is the eternal Presence of God.

Smiling snaps me out of my stupor of thinking that just because I don't feel God's presence that God isn't present...right here, right now.

Smiling alerts me to the larger tasks of life, discovering and incorporating my over-arching purpose of living.

Smiling stirs in the sweetness of the relationship between God and me.

Smiling helps me see the light that the darkness of aloneness is never abandonment.

Smiling jogs my focus back to the center-point of my soul.

Don't cry because it's over, smile because it happened.

Dr. Suess

Endnote

I think it appropriate to end this little volume with the lyrics of a song that has perhaps been recorded by more contemporary artists than "Jingle Bells."

Can you sing the song in your head?

Smile

Smile though your heart is aching;

    smile even though it's breaking.

When there are clouds in the sky, you'll get by.

If you smile through your fear and sorrow,

    smile and maybe tomorrow,

    you'll see the sun come shining through for you.

Light up your face with gladness.

Hide every trace of sadness,

    although a tear may be ever so near.

That's the time you must keep on trying,

    smile what's the use of crying.

You'll find that life is still worthwhile,

    if you just smile.

        (Public domain: Chaplin/Turner/Parsons)

References

Peale, Norman Vincent, The Power of Positive Thinking, 1952.

Maddi, Salvatore and Suzanne Kobasa, The Hardy Executive: Health Under Stress Dow Jones-Irwin, Homewood, IL, 1984.

Seligman, Martin, Learned Optimism, How to Change Your Mind and Your Life, 1992.

Morrison, James, DSM-IV Made Easy, Guilford Press, New York, 1995.

Norville, Deborah, Thank You Power: Making the Science of Gratitude Work for You, 2008.

Johnson, Richard, P., Discover Your Spiritual Strengths, AGES Press, St. Louis, MO, 2008.

All quotes are taken from the Application (app) "Notable Quotes" iPhone edition.

Made in the USA
Middletown, DE
18 November 2021